Once upon a time:
How Cinderella Grew Up and Became a Happy Empowered Woman

By Sandra Reich & Maïté Gomez

ISBN: 1479182672
ISBN 13: 9781479182671

"Sandra Reich and Maïté Gomez take women on a wonderful journey out of the traps that block relationship happiness and onto the road of satisfying relationships: "*How Cinderella Grew Up and Became a Happy Empowered Woman*" teaches women to master the strategies of the dance of relationships from two experts in the field"

'Dr Laurie Betito
Psychologist, Sex Therapist and Radio Host

"We all know the tale of the brave hero rescuing the distressed princess. My industry is responsible for perpetuating that annoying cliché, and unfortunately little girls and grown women the world over cling to it. Well, it took thirty-five years and oodles of therapy before I realized the truth: I need to be the hero in my own life! But now the journey to empowerment has just gotten easier. *Once upon a time-How Cinderella Grew Up and Became a Happy Empowered Woman* offers a brave new path where anything is possible - and the best part, it's all up to us. With clarity, compassion and sharp insight, Reich and Gomez break down everything we THOUGHT we knew about love, relationships and ourselves. They demystify and deconstruct all of those bumps that impede our quest for happiness. This must be mandatory reading for every woman, especially teenagers, because we all deserve to "live happily ever after!"

'Tracey Deer- Gemini Award Winning Film Director

"*Once upon a time how Cinderella Grew up and Became a Happy Empowered Woman*" teaches concepts that can dramatically change women's lives. Sandra and Maïté have successfully and efficiently used fairy tale metaphors to highlight dangerous patterns that women fall into, (that show up in my practice daily) and written down solutions in a self-help book that can dramatically change women's lives and relationships. This is a "must read" for any woman and especially any woman who has had challenges in their relationships (and who has not?). The path to being a happy empowered woman involves understanding and overcoming set ups that block the way so you can live the life of your dreams. This book has a serious hard core road map written out for you. You will be amazed from the moment you open page one – **you** will see **yourself**, your **patterns** and **find solutions**. You will not be able to put this one down. If you are a woman, "*Once upon a time how Cinderella Grew up and Became a Happy Empowered Woman*" is a must read.

'Solline Feld M.A, M.F.T
Psychologist

About the Authors

Sandra Reich

Sandra Reich, M.Ed, is the Clinical Director of the Montreal Center for Anxiety and Depression as well as Co-director of Empowered Women Workshops. She has been working in the field of behavioral and eclectic therapy for over fourteen years. She is a well-known specialist in the fields of anxiety, depression, self-esteem, emotional work and relationships. She has dedicated her life to understanding behaviors, human nature, people's love lives, and relationships in general. She has done extensive training in these areas and has been featured on The Discovery Health Channel, APTN and Global amongst others as an expert on these topics. Sandra is a popular radio personality, keynote speaker and known as a top relationship and anxiety expert.

Maïté Gomez

Maïté Gomez holds a degree in psychology (Université de Montréal, 1993) and a degree in psycho-corporelle intégrée (Body-mind counseling, Hito, 1999); she is also a licensed massage therapist (Shiatsu and Swedish, Guijek, 2000) and a somatic practitioner (Gymnastique Émotionelle®, 2012). She is Co-director of Empowered Women Workshops and has been in private practice since 1999. She has devoted her life to understanding the body-mind-spirit connection and the natural healing processes through different modalities. Maïté is versed in traditional Chinese medicine, integrated body-psychology, and bio-mechanic and somatic bodywork.

Table of Contents

Acknowledgments

We would like specially to thank the following people who have been our teachers, our inspirations, and our guides.

Our moms: Suzanne and Ginette, J.G., Oprah, S.F., Eli, Ron, Danielle, Hersh, Carolyne, Melodie Beattie, Martin, our clients who never stop inspiring us, our partners: Mark and David, for their support and our children, for whom we build and dream of a loving world.

Introduction

We had both been in private practice for many years when the idea of the Empowered Women Workshops first came up. We had also been in committed relationships, raising children, and had encountered many of the challenges modern women face. We decided to work together after discussing the common themes that showed up in our cases, as well as our own similar challenges. From these elements, the workshops to empower women were born. From these common themes we found conclusive answers and strategies that can help the modern woman understand the choices available to her while still feeling good about herself.

Though the research and intensity of the topics were huge, the answers were relatively simple. Yet for the hundreds of women we worked with, applying our solutions often felt counterintuitive. We plunged further in, to understand more, and slowly but surely, the stuff that felt so counterintuitive was pretty logical after all.

It seemed that we, as women, had forgotten basic biology, adaptations, gender differences and the importance of self-love. We had not been strongly encouraged towards the concept of self-love, and yet it is the single most important ingredient to our own happiness. Further, our society strongly reinforces a concept, particularly in women's minds, called *caretaking*, which often benefits everyone but women.

In addition to this, women are subtly encouraged to be hard on each other for the presumably valued and coveted male attention As this is not disadvantageous to men- it is (unconsciously at times) reinforced by them and by society.

Women's roles continue to evolve. The women's liberation movement allowed women to take on many new roles. Women joined the ranks of those in the corporate world as agents of change, movers and shakers, executives and top professionals. This was wonderful but as the roles grew many women lost themselves more and more. Being considered a good multi-tasker is taken as a compliment, and yet multitasking has chipped away at our ability to experience joy and balance.

Many of the women we met were at the top of their game. They were brilliant, beautiful, deep, insightful, and yet they appeared to be suffering. Very often, managing interpersonal relationships was at the heart of much of their suffering.

Thus, Empowered Women Workshops was born. We started giving one-day lectures. We compiled what we had learned, practiced, and taught our principles successfully to many women. This grew into our retreats for intensive learning.

The response at our workshops was amazing. The energy in the room was beyond touching. Women were coming together, supporting each other, learning from each other and reaching for the stars.

Following these great moments, we decided to put pen to paper and show women how to apply our concepts to their daily lives.

We do feel it is important to start this book mentioning that ultimately *you* are the biggest expert regarding your life, so these thoughts are for your consideration only. We ask that you, to please ask yourself what is right for you and decide what can be helpful or not for you.

Furthermore, our field of expertise surrounds heterosexual relationships so that is where our focus will be in this book; though we suspect that many of these concepts could be applied to same sex relationships as well.

We would love to meet you at one of our day events or at a multiday retreat. We hold full-day events in Montreal yearly, and two retreats are also held yearly at an amazing spa where we delve into our intensive program. Should you want to attend one of these wonderfully transformative programs, please visit our website at www.empoweredwomenworkshops.com for further information.

Once Upon a Time

Once upon a time, there was a woman. She had choices like no other woman before her.

She could choose the usual choices that her sisters, mothers, and aunts had chosen before her. She could choose to live the same roles the women of her clan had lived for generations, or she could choose to go out on a limb and explore new horizons. All the choices were in front of her:

Wife
Lover
Mother
Friend
Leader
Teacher
Provider
Nurturer

There was all of this to consider and all that she had yet to imagine.

What was she to choose? And, most important of all, why and how could she embrace her choices?

Behind each choice and role lurked the power of the story given by the preceding generations. She could embody a role with her innate sense of empowerment, or she could be a servant to the role. Only by lifting the veil of her inner dialogue, revealing its light and shadows, could she learn to navigate her choices and not be a servant to the power and wills of others.

On her search for her true power and true self, she discovered that there were choices preceding those roles to create her life and happiness.

As a woman, her biology had created a certain reality that was part of the truth she had to honor to build herself steadily.

Prior to fulfilling her chosen roles, she had to choose the role of her power, her inner voice.

A whole new reality had emerged. She had first to learn the truth of who she was and the truth of her power, before she was ever to consider living in happiness and peace with her other roles.

She felt both the excitement and the weight of her discovery. She had found answers. Those answers demanded that she go deep within to find a new truth, to explore, to be introspective, to commit, and to act according to those new, emerging truths.

She felt the burden of the world even as she wondered how and why she had discovered such a well of wisdom within, when at the same time, it felt so heavy on her shoulders.

Taking a deep breath, she rose. She looked around, observing. She had spent many days wondering, observing this world and the people in it, and contemplating their choices and actions. She couldn't decide yet whether she would embark on the journey.

Until one day—the day her eyes locked on the eyes of a sister—and right away, she knew…

She knew this woman knew what she was experiencing.
She, too, was searching.
She, too, was struggling.
She, too, wanted more.

She knew that, just like her, this woman wanted to be free.

Taking a big breath, she realized that she had found her courage to plunge.

"I will not be alone in this journey," she said. "I will not let you be alone either."

At that moment, the sky and the earth opened with a promise: "We only need for you to commit to your power and to your journey. From now on, neither of you will ever be alone again."

Psychobiology of Men and Women

There are biological realities associated with the roles men and women have. As we wrote this book it seemed very clear to us that ignoring these realities would be a disservice to the women who read it.

One of the fundamental truths about human nature is that we love in the way we want to be loved. It makes sense to think that if you treat the one you love the way you would like to be loved, you will receive that love in return. But it really does not work that way in human relationships.

Men and women are wired very differently; our brains are different and our adaptations are different. We receive love differently, we appreciate differently, and we value differently.

Much research concerning these differences has been done in the field of psychology. Some of the most fascinating research on this topic comes from biological anthropologist Dr. Helen Fisher, who talks a lot in her research about the hunter-gatherer adaptations from the time of cave dwellers and how our brains have plasticized accordingly.

For centuries women were gatherers. Their primary role was to stay with other women to sort out food and to gather anything we could to keep our families alive (not so different from now).

While women gathered, men primarily worked as hunters. Hunting was highly valued and a good hunter made a good partner.

We know that brain wiring gets a lot of strength from repetition and reinforcement, a process that is referred to as malleable yet fundamental hardwiring. From studying early human behavior, we can hypothesize that men's desire to hunt is somewhat wired into their way of thinking. We like to refer to this phenomenon in a way that our female clients integrate well, by saying that most men value what they have to work (or hunt) for, and they do not cherish what they do not have to work for.

This presents a huge problem for women, especially for "caretaking" women. Caretakers derive great pleasure in making other people's lives easier. The true caretaking woman is low-maintenance and is usually very proud of that. However, if men are hunters and value what they work for, what happens to that woman? Is she cherished? She should be because of her considerate, thoughtful and selfless nature. Unfortunately she is usually treated with disregard while non-caretaking women (sometimes unpleasantly referred to as the B word) are often pursued.

Ironically, the devoted caretaker is typically the woman who shows up in therapy with anxiety or depression and usually with a series of disappointing relationships and deep battle scars. Underneath the pain she wonders where she went wrong.

When working with such a client we usually start by asking this type of woman what kind of makeup she wears. If she does not wear makeup, we discuss the type of jewelry she likes, and if she does not wear jewelry, then we discuss which handbags she likes—whatever it is that she really loves and that makes her feel beautiful and valuable. In each instance the woman ultimately describes an expensive brand of lipstick, such as Chanel or Lancôme, or tells how much she loves her diamond ring, or how she treasures her Coach handbag. We then will ask her if she gives equal treatment and loving care to a lipstick from the dollar store, a cubic zirconium ring, or a knock-off handbag. Which one does she treat better? There is usually a look of realization combined with a touch of horror as she realizes what is being asked of her and the reality of what her answers mean.

The bottom line is that we all valuc what we work for, and therefore, we value more expensive things because we've had to work harder to attain them. We do not treat the drugstore lipstick the same as the Dior lipstick. We do not take care of the cubic zirconium ring the same way we do the diamond, and we throw around the knock-off purse, not worried that it might get too worn-out looking, while we carefully and lovingly take care of the "Coach" bag. These practices almost do not make sense except for the cold, hard reality that working hard increases the pleasure of the reward.

This phenomenon is much stronger in men as it dates back to their cavemen-hunter days. Men traditionally shown tremendous value for items they had to "hunt" or work hard for. Nowadays such items might include the beautiful home or the car and stereo system. Included in this might also include more non-material items such as their love interest. Therefore as counterintuitive as it may sound, being a low-maintenance woman who goes out of her way to make her man's life easier does not increase his love meter for her. The opposite may in fact be true. It is in the modern woman's best interest to ensure that men work for her time and affection.

When we discuss this with our clients, they often say, "Well, don't ask me to start playing games now…" Is this a game? Is being a diamond a game? Or is being a diamond simply being your true and ideal self?

Reducing the light in ourselves and "playing small," as Marianne Williamson puts it in her brilliant poem, "Our Deepest Fear," is not healthy for us at all.

Our deepest fear is not that we are inadequate.
Our deepest fear is that we are powerful beyond measure.
It is our light, not our darkness
That most frightens us.
Your playing small
Does not serve the world.
There's nothing enlightened about shrinking
So that other people won't feel insecure around you.

We are all meant to shine,
As children do.
We were born to make manifest
The glory of God that is within us.

It's not just in some of us;
It's in everyone.

And as we let our own light shine,
We unconsciously give other people permission to do the same.
As we're liberated from our own fear,
Our presence automatically liberates others.[1]

Shining our light is the ultimate goal. Yet we often play ourselves down. If women do not want to be treated like dollar store lipstick, how and why do we end up acting that way?

This problem starts early in our lives. People tell us what we are missing and how we could be better. We have the added bonus of being subtly but repeatedly reminded that each woman's prize for being good enough will be the approval of a man. We are set up to believe from an early age that our own value is somehow not enough. Messages from mass media bombard women on an hourly basis regarding the perfect look and life. It's no secret that super models are photo shopped to look more desirable. Now that we use computer aided graphics to create the image of the perfect woman, the standard by which millions of women hold themselves to is completely out of reach. Add to this society's pressure for women to find the perfect man, to play the part, and to conform to what is considered the right way to look, act, and be, we end up creating a society full of women with disastrous self-esteem issues manifested as eating disorders, emotional distress, anxiety and undeveloped coping strategies to name but a few.

The idea of coupling with a partner is a nice concept and we take no objection to this. But it is a two-way street. Men get to couple with us and yet men are not raised to think that their value is solely based on looking good enough or being good enough to find a suitable partner.

In our counseling sessions, we have found that men do struggle with other challenges and issues related to finding a mate. When it comes to loving and treating themselves well, however, they are typically much better at this than women are. So the deck is stacked right from the start. As women we still worry about being high-maintenance when we practice good self-care and, even worse that we might be guilty of playing a game with men if we expect to be treated as a rare gem. Men value what they work for. We need to value ourselves enough to let them work in order to win our hearts and our love.

None of us starts life thinking we are zircon or flawed in any way do we? Yet when we think of such things as owning our own value, being not overly low-maintenance, and refraining from caretaking, we think of these things as "playing a game."

Allowing someone you love to enjoy what fuels his or her love for you seems to be a win/win strategy for everyone. Understanding life strategy is a key component to this life "game" we are all in.

We are always amazed by the allergic reaction most women have to what they perceive as game playing. The reality is we all actually do play some games. We like to say we do not, and we pride ourselves on our direct honesty, but we all have unwritten codes we live by that have inherent games within them. All of us actually do play games in life, as life is more than a bit of a game.

If you do not agree with that statement, we could simply discuss courtship in its many forms and we would find games on several levels. Is makeup not a game to increase one's sex appeal? Flirtation? Playing hard to get? Being low-maintenance? Selectively revealing our pasts? These are all technically games. We have to be careful not to fall into our righteous position that "we do not play games." We would like to propose to you that we all play games of some sort and that perhaps a game that is win/win for everyone involved should be considered a good game.

Since we have suggested that men value what they work for, then what type of man does a low-maintenance woman attract and usually end up with? Due to her care-taking efforts this type of woman usually spends much of her energy helping those at home, at work and around the community. She works each day in the service of others on a conscious and unconscious level, depleting herself of vital energy. It is highly likely the man in her life will happily feed off that energy, meaning that she will likely attract or create a narcissistic man or, at minimum, will indirectly encourage narcissism.

Furthermore, if the man in this woman's life sees that she does not value herself, he may conclude at some unconscious level that she must not be of significant value. Not only does he treat her as someone who isn't of much value, his attention can quickly turn to a woman who loves herself enough to treat herself as a diamond.

Sadly, this is often the case when we hear of a very "nice" woman, who has done everything for "her man", being left for the "other woman" often referred to as the "bitch". We have encountered this scenario repeatedly in our practices. Does it mean that being a "bitch" pays off? Not exactly; **being a woman who values herself pays off.**

We like nice woman and we want you to remain a nice woman, but we want you to see your value and to be careful when giving yourself and your heart away too easily. Men need the pleasure of working for you. This is what they biologically want to do, so this is not anti-feminism as much as it is straight psychobiology.

Another factor to consider is that men often become restless or annoyed when not working towards a goal. Women inevitably see this type of man as non-cherishing and passive-aggressive. He may in fact not be happy with the feeling that he does not have to work for his diamond. This is unconscious, of course. But why deprive him of this joy? Why deprive yourself of feeling like a diamond?

On any given night, we see men watching sporting events. Why do sports appeal to so many men? When we think of sports in terms of men being hunters, we know the answer. Athletic events involve a chase, be it chasing a small puck on the ice or a football across a field. Men are hunters. You just cannot fight psychobiology, so why try?

A common question many women ask is, "Do I have to play hard to get forever?" The answer is, *Not at all.* The goal is not **"playing hard to get"** it is simply **reclaiming** your own value and importance. You are merely setting the tone for the relationship and your own psychological health. Respect yourself and he will respect you. Disrespect yourself early on in the relationship and it becomes doomed for failure before it even had a chance to succeed.

Love without respect dies.

Relationships that start with mutual trust and respect, where both parties hold themselves to a higher standard, typically last much longer. If you respect yourself and command respect, you are much more likely to have more intimate and satisfying interpersonal relationships. To respect yourself you must love yourself. Loving yourself is the single most important key to your own happiness. By loving yourself first and foremost you naturally become the diamond you were meant to be. This makes you happy and makes him happy too- win/win.

If this is not a big enough motivation to get out of the caretaking dance, here is another one. When we are busy giving our energy to someone, we are draining our own energy. Another way of looking at this energy drain could be as a **De-press-ion.**

Who suffers from depression the most? Women suffer depression close to twice as much as men do. This might, in fact, be (partly) related to the naturally slippery slope of caretaking as discussed earlier. If you try to give to another without self-care, you deplete your energy reserves. Giving away your energy is a surefire recipe for a physical or psychological symptom to appear. Further, depleting yourself will naturally invite a repression of emotions (perhaps anger) and a repression of emotions tends to lead one to being susceptible to symptoms of depression or anxiety in particular. So not practicing self-care is really quite dangerous in terms of your own psychological health.

This chapter wouldn't be complete without discussing another biological difference between men and women: Sex. Many of us watched and loved Samantha's character on the television show, *Sex and the City.* She was proud to be a prowler "like a man", she was determined to be detached "like a man" and she was not going to get hurt "like women do." Samantha took great pride in her single status, free to come and go as she pleased, trying to remain detached and irreverent during much of her adult dating life. As much as she may have tried to act as a stereotypical single male, Samantha's biology dictated otherwise.

Samantha was a woman, and ultimately, she was very hurt by many men. Why couldn't even Samantha beat biology? Men can prowl and have multiple partners and not get as attached as women do, but why?

In a word: oxytocin. What is oxytocin? It is sometimes referred to as the love hormone. Oxytocin is crucial to attachment and attachment is crucial to love. One of the key things we know about oxytocin is that it is released in large doses while women breastfeed. It actually bonds the child with the mother and the mother with the child. It is nature's attempt at guaranteeing a secure bond between mom and child.

Here is the kicker in all of this: during sex, women produce lots of oxytocin, a hormone that stimulates a strong emotional connection. As a result, women get more emotionally attached when it comes to sex.

That's why casual sex and "quickie" hookups backfire for most women. Men also produce oxytocin but men's oxytocin's levels are affected by different factors then women's are, so they are more likely to have the option to have sex with less emotional connection. This is not to say that they cannot emotionally attach—they can, and they do. But they can also have casual sex without attachment more easily than women can.

Psychobiology rears its head once again. The deck is stacked. Women who are trying to be like the sexually detached male are set up to fail because even though their wills are strong, their biology is stronger. Oxytocin will cause the attachment to form. Attaching during sex means we are starting on the road to possibly "fall in love" and we know where that fall leads, which is wonderful once we know **who** we are risking all of this for. Unfortunately, however, on far too many occasions we do not.

In Steve Harvey's wonderful book, *Act like a Lady, Think like a Man*, he suggests that when a woman first meets a man she is interested in, she should wait ninety days before having sex with him.[2] Many modern day women might read this and think, "*Wow, this is really old school advice. We are modern women. We can have sex whenever we want…right?*" Yes, but we are going to become attached due to our friend, oxytocin. "OK, but so what? He seems so nice, after all…"

Becoming attached might be best once we know to whom we are becoming attached to. Steve Harvey points out that even when we start new jobs, a certain amount of time passes (usually approximately ninety days) before we are able to earn benefits, since our employers don't know who we are yet, and they need time to develop trust in us before giving us benefits. Harvey muses in his book about women, wondering why women give their trust, their hearts, and their bodies before knowing who their sexual partners are. We think that is a brilliant question!

Since oxytocin binds us to our sexual partners, which leads to feelings of attachment, should a woman not consider waiting until she knows whether this man is a viable risk for her emotional well-being?

Our hearts, our bodies, and the deepest parts of **ourselves** are sacred and special. Heartbreak is no fun, as anyone who has suffered the experience will tell you. There are no guarantees against heartbreak, but making sure you are not risking those very special parts of yourself with someone you are unsure of is a smart way to protect your heart. Becoming attached to someone is a beautiful concept when you have found someone who is worthy of that attachment. Taking the time to get to know, trust and respect each other is possibly the most exciting part of any new relationship. Steve Harvey suggests 90 days – we are not sure of exact timing, but giving yourself this time may be the singular most important gift you can give to yourself to evaluate if your love interest is a real gem or just a fake.

Biology is always at play in love relationships. It is a reality between men and women. Understanding psychobiology is a gift to oneself—accepting it is nirvana.

Victim

Women and the Role of Victim

Becoming dominant first in North America and Western Europe more than one hundred and fifty years ago, the movement for equality between men and women has spread throughout the world. As with all social movements, it is stronger in certain areas and is still in great need of growth in others.

Being involved in this movement is not a question of being feminist. For many of us, when our grandmothers were born, women had only recently been granted the right to vote. We must honor the fight for equality our mothers, grandmothers, and great-grandmothers fought for. We believe theirs was the most honorable fight of all. They fought for equal rights and opportunities for generations to come, quite often risking their own safety and that of their families.

Because of their efforts, women in many countries today share in all legal rights, liberties and freedom as men do. Combine education with legal rights and you raise the level of consciousness and the quality of life for all members within that society.

The fight against victimization is not a new one, either for us as a nation or for us as daughters of women who fought for equal opportunity. You may even have encountered situations where you yourself had to pick up the battle for equality.

In spite of all the progress made by women around the world the questions remains why do we still fall into victim roles?

The Inner Dialogue of the Victim

In the previous section we looked briefly at the role of women in history and the feminist movement.

The role of women changed very quickly with the onset of the industrial revolution. Women began working outside of the home more frequently; some became the sole bread-winner. Women were allowed the right to vote and run for political office. Women were for the first time equal partners in nearly all aspects of society.

Despite all the positive changes which took place, there is still a battle being fought within the female psyche. The first battle involves victimization. How so? Let us first define what a victim is in this scenario.

In *Encarta*, a digital encyclopedia formerly published and maintained by Microsoft, a victim is defined as "a **helpless person:** somebody who experiences misfortune and feels helpless to remedy it."

According to *Wiktionary.org*[3]

A victim is:

-Anyone who is harmed by another

-An aggrieved or disadvantaged party in a crime

-A person who suffers any other injury, loss, or damage as a result of a voluntary undertaking.

-An unfortunate person who suffers from a disaster or other adverse circumstance.

We have all felt victimized at some point in our lives. When was the last time you had an injustice perpetrated against you? Was it malicious, intentional or impersonal?

There is one undeniable truth about a victim. There is no victim without a perpetrator, even if the perpetrator is fate, bad luck, or life itself.

Who or what is to blame for an injustice? The victim, in the state of victimhood, is the innocent. When we say that someone has fallen victim to a situation, we are saying that person is innocent, clear of blame, and cannot be made accountable or responsible for what has happened.

The one who is granted the title of "victim" is cleared of all blame. We then look elsewhere to assign the burden of blame. Whatever, or whomever, caries the blame is the perpetrator. This is a dance that frequently gets played out in relationships.

We are not responsible. So the blame goes to:

Bad luck
Our parents

Our sibling(s)
Our spouses
The society we live in,
Our astrological signs,
Life itself or
(Sadly we often even blame) Our children

When we adopt this way of viewing and living life, the perpetrators are as numerous as the victims. The truth in all of this is that life is not fair, but things get easier once we accept this reality.

Our internal dialogue rages, "*It's not fair, life is not fair, and it was supposed to be fair*!" Unfortunately by adopting this form of inner dialogue we clear a path towards a life of victimization.

Princesses of Inner Dialogue

Oh, girls! Oh, little girls, who is the princess you prefer? Which one of them do you long to be?

Is it Cinderella, covered in ashes and dust, in her torn garments? Poor Cinderella, slaving for her stepmother, humiliated by her stepsisters and all this because she had the misfortune to lose her mother to illness! Her father, lacking in character and fortitude, let his new wife turn his firstborn into a servant, befriended only by the birds and the vermin of the house.

From out of thin air, her fairy Godmother gives her the gift of all gifts; the chance to go to the royal ball, complete with a magnificent dress, glass shoes, and a carriage. There, out of all the young women in the kingdom, the prince chooses her, and they dance all night, intoxicated with each other. She flees at midnight ensuring the prince will not have to learn of her true lot in life. She vanishes, and he pursues her, aided by the glass shoe she left behind.

As the story goes he soon finds her, rescues her from her evil stepsisters and stepmother, marries her, and loves her forever after. No more struggles for Cinderella.

Although it appears to be a lovely children's story with wonderful lessons about treating others with respect, the message Cinderella sends to young ladies may not be the right one.

The initial lesson we'd like to teach about the women in this story is the value of solidarity. As women we must unite and present a strong unified bond.

When women turn on each other, there is no one left to trust. Psychology suggests to us that women hating women is really just women hating themselves. If we turn on each other, we are sure to turn on ourselves. What prevents you from becoming the perpetrator? If you can be someone else's perpetrator, then you can surely be your own.

We would also knock on the fairy godmother's door to ask her what she was thinking in telling Cinderella to believe that a fancy ball and a marriage to a prince would make her happy forever. What does the reader get from this story? Do we think the fairy godmother, with all her power, is giving Cinderella the best advice she can? What about educating her father and Cinderella, not to mention the stepmother and the stepdaughters? So many questions left unanswered. So many issues unresolved.

Above all else we mustn't ignore where Cinderella searched for her self-worth: In the affections of a man. Cinderella, as a heroine, must be the creator of her own self-esteem, confidence and worth. Cinderella's true happiness lies in seeing herself for all that she is a beautiful, smart, caring woman. The essence of her happiness must begin with the relationship she has with herself.

How much more powerful and impactful would the story have been if Cinderella had focused on her own goals and personal needs? How different and ultimately more interesting would the story have been if she had had been cautious with the Prince, expecting that he "court" her for a time, demonstrating his love in other ways whilst she considers how this feels about him. Her worth had nothing to do with romance- it was her own, from the moment she was born. Your worth is yours as your birthright, too.

Though the fairy tale does not send this message, Cinderella's worth was the same when she was unkempt and doing her stepmother's chores as it was when the prince pursued and married her. Your worth cannot change for the better or for the worse. You must always believe you are worthy. If you are struggling with your self-worth you may want to try the Adlerian "act as if" method. Begin to "act as if" you believe you are worthy, talk "as if" you believe you are worthy and respond "as if" you are always worthy. For some, developing a strong sense of self takes a great deal of time and for others it happens more quickly. Be kind to yourself. Prince Charming may make you feel better, but that is temporary. You goal isn't temporary. Only you can ultimately make you feel better. It is the only known method to keep the light strong when difficult times come your way.

By learning to love ourselves we can more easily learn to love our fellow sisters and brothers. The first person we need to fully empower is the person looking back from the mirror. If we remove our power, it becomes reasonable to assume that others can also take away our power and authority. If you know your worth from the beginning, you have a voice against injustice—you can set boundaries and command respect. You will be a powerful, empowered woman. The chances of you being treated well in relationships skyrockets as opposed to the situation for the woman who seeks her self-worth externally.

The romanticism of Cinderella, as the victim who is saved by a Prince, feeds right into the "seductiveness of victimization". This concept deserves some further explanation.

For many the victim mindset is an attractive one because it removes all responsibility and accountability. As a victim, one can live with the mantra "it's not my fault." Life becomes a series of events that happens to the victim, without purpose and without responsibility, but with devastating consequences. Typically, victims attract perpetrators. They are drawn to each other like moths to a flame. Much of the work is done on a very unconscious level hence many victims feel they carry no responsibility or accountability. Unhealthy and failed relationships seem to "just happen" time and time again. If you press for answers you simply get, "I don't know. These things just seem to happen to me. I keep picking the wrong man, the wrong friends or the wrong job". In general those who live with a power mindset see the world entirely differently. They keep their inner circle very tight, their relationships tend to last longer (if fulfilling), they make friends for life and they tend to be fulfilled by their careers.

In the context of Cinderella, as a "victim" attracts and marries her Prince. The victim didn't attract the expected perpetrator, hence the beauty of a fairytale. In reality, as stated earlier, victims attract perpetrators. Ask yourself this question: In what world do you live in? Are you accountable, responsible and control of your destiny? Or do you choose to live in a world like Cinderella's, a world where you're only hope is to be rescued by a charming Prince?

To see how this subtle message is sent to our little girls time and time again, let's look at another famous fairy tale.

Snow White: she's as pretty and white as snow, and of course there's the evil stepmother. (What a shocker! No female solidarity yet again…)

The older, evil stepmom is jealous of her stepdaughter's beauty, but why? The Stepmother has the title, the money, and the magic. Does she need eternal youth too? It does raise the assumption that youth and beauty play a vital role in how we value ourselves. She is a woman with power, but in fairy tales such a person is called a witch. Women can be nothing but corrupt if you give them power. She will turn dark, greedy, and deadly. Ouch! We all know these fairytale equations by now:

Prince = Hero
Princess = (Attractive) Victim
Woman of power = Evil, envious, bad witch

The stepmother contracts a hunter to slay the princess by removing her beating heart. The stepdaughter is too pretty a thing to kill and is spared by the hunter. She flees into the forest and is rescued by seven men. She escapes her evil stepmother by living with those seven men, for whom she cleans and cooks. As the evil stepmom is actually an evil witch, she poisons an apple and tricks Snow White into eating it. The seven men are devastated.

A prince passes by, and when he kisses the lifeless beauty, she comes back to life, and off they go on his valiant horse.

Snow White, the victim who is saved by her beauty and innocence (yes, the hunter spared her life), is aided by seven men in the woods and saved by a prince and a kiss!

Now let's consider the fairy tale about Sleeping Beauty. This story yet again follows the same formula of

Prince = Hero,
Princess = Victim,
Woman of power = Evil, envious, bad witch.

The princess is young and pretty. The woman of power is older, jealous, cold and calculating, with psychopathic tendencies.

The woman of power puts a spell on the whole castle via the princess' finger. They all sleep for a hundred years.

A prince passes by and the woman of power transforms herself into a dragon. The prince kills the dragon. The prince finds the princess, kisses her, and she awakes! She is saved, married, and happy for eternity.

Sleeping Beauty, a victimized girl, is saved by a prince and a kiss—once again, the same message.

Can anyone blame any of us for falling prey to the seduction of the victim consciousness at one point or another? We were practically raised on it.

We've been taught since we were little girls, through our favorite stories, that what you need to do is just be a (hopefully pretty) victim, and the world will fall at your feet. Kisses and princes are all we need, along with the promise of forever after plenitude.

But seek power, and you'll turn into a witch.

Seek the victim consciousness and you are sure to be saved. Someone in this universe will sense your innocence and go out of his way to come and rescue you, pledging his love and the rest of his life to you. And you will need this—since you cannot save yourself.

If there is one premise to all the work we do and to this book, it is that you definitely can save yourself. We urge our clients and you, our readers, not to buy into this *romantic fantasy* that steals your self-esteem and worthiness and puts them into the hands of another.

The Emotional Victim

"It's not fair! It's not my fault."
"I am just not good enough."

This sentiment can lead you to the pinnacle of emotional victimhood, complete with trumpets, red carpets and happy endings. After all, the fairy-tale told you this was the magic recipe: be a victim, "innocent, quiet, and helpless". Be a victim, and you'll stay pure, be saved, get treated fairly and all that your heart desires. Once you adopt this sentiment, if anything goes wrong, it is followed by the belief that you do not have control over your own circumstances and that if things are off it is because the world is against you. The questions and beliefs swirl in your mind: "Why me?" "I am powerless." "I have no choice." "Yes, but…" (The authors' personal favorite) and, "Everyone is out to get me." Those are just a few. If you find yourself often repeating those phrases you are likely already operating from a victim mindset perhaps without even realizing it.

We may catch someone or ourselves harboring these beliefs. Certain circumstances are out of our control. The question is how long we choose to dwell on them. That part belongs to us and is in our control.

How many times is the sting of injustice felt?

As a society, it is true we believe and defend equal opportunity. Life does intervene with its own set of mysterious rules and sometimes they hardly feel fair at all. Some people are born prettier, smarter, richer, stronger, or with better parents.

Thus, from the belief that fairness is a primary rule of life, we can sometimes become emotional victims due to our belief that if our circumstances had been different, our lives would have been better and happier. This makes us long for something that hasn't manifested in our lives.

What we do next is crucial.

If you feel that a negative situation cannot be changed, whether due to fate or because you feel powerless, you may stay stuck in the circular logic that is feeding your feelings of helplessness and making them stay alive. This plan was good enough for the fairy princesses—why not for you?

You'll then likely be drawn into the "It's not fair! It's not my fault!" mentality.

People can debate the topic of fairness for hours— maintaining how life really is unfair. If you are born into poverty, do you have the same opportunities as those who are born into wealth? Some would argue if you are born with a physical condition that impairs your physical movements, diminishes your life expectancy, and limits your mental capacity, then many opportunities will not be possible.

Who could argue that these things are fair?

The real question is not to decide the fairness of one's life. The real question is *how* you view your circumstances and *what* you do about them.

Will you search for a perpetrator—someone or something to blame? Doing so will propel you toward the role of the victim. As an innocent, you will be out of reach of either blame or rcsponsibility and thus out of reach of your own power and strength.

There are huge advantages to staying in the role of the victim. What does one have to gain by feeling "victimized by unfairness?"

The Deeper River

What could we possibly gain by giving in to the victim mentality?

Attention

When we engage people with our troubles, we are enabling the victim mind-set by gaining attention from them and gaining their sympathy for our plight. Of course, this is not to say that there is anything wrong with confiding in a close friend and sitting down to vent and find solutions.

However, what if we introduce ourselves in the following manner, "Oh! I'm doing so-so, all things considered. I am tired, and I miss my brother, who lives abroad. Life is just so difficult. I haven't been able to see him and this feels so unfair when I see so many brothers and sisters together here."

Saying this kind of interaction exemplifies victim mentality may seem harsh but consider the alternative:

"All in all I am doing well but I will confide something to you. I've been working very hard on gratitude. Even to be healthy is such a blessing and I had forgotten about that. So I am now working on being thankful and slowing down. I want to go to see my brother. I have not been able to gather all the money yet, but I'm doing it bit by bit and staying positive. I found this great new thing. Do you know about Skype? I'm in better spirits now that I've taken time to speak to and see my brother on Skype. How lucky we are. We're so far away but we have the technology to stay close!"

Sympathy

We have seen that people's hearts bleed for victims. Be a victim of a situation and you will find someone to take pity on you. You are then safely in the land of no responsibility. You have pity and sympathy and as a bonus good feelings have been extended toward you. People have given you a pass to avoid whatever it is you have wanted to avoid.

Avoidance of responsibility and avoidance of action

At other times, we couldn't care less about sympathy. But we could be struck by fear, grief, or stubbornness and be absolutely prepared for inaction.

We can avoid talking about the situation, avoid taking responsibility for our part and avoid what would be the action that would get us going in the right direction.

When we are victims, inaction and avoidance are worn as a badge of "how bad something is" in order to alert others to our need for assistance.

The Markers Encrusted in the Victim Mentality

It is not a question of whether we will venture into the territory of the victim consciousness, but of when we will do so and how long we will stay there.

There are clues to help us know when we are entering the victim mentality.

In the victim mentality, everything becomes a struggle.

If you are struggling with everything in life and you have been doing so for a long time, this is a sign that should be paid attention to.

How we create our own helplessness.

Having a victim mentality could potentially break your will. Staying in that frame of mind will, over time, deplete energy required to prevail over challenging circumstances such as divorce, bankruptcy or something as little as cleaning a cluttered basement.

It might indeed be possible for some to shift from this particular set of circumstances, but if you tell yourself it is not possible you will remain in the same set circumstances, creating more clutter, drama and helplessness.

When you feel helpless, you're in victim mode.

Victims believe they have little capacity to take care of themselves.

This can come from believing one lacks the resources to accomplish something. This could include lack of energy, lack of friends, family, money, social status—choose an excuse.

This feeling of having limited capacity always comes from the silent belief that this situation is too hard. It really shouldn't be that hard to take care of oneself…right?

Victims are subject to a distorted reality.

Once we take on the victim consciousness, even the way we talk and think is tainted, sometimes to the point where we lose contact with reality and the possibilities at hand. The way we view our situations becomes very circular. No matter the argument presented we are locked into our positions. No matter the solution presented, we have a "Yes, but…" as an answer. We are stuck and stagnant, with no way out.

Although blocking solutions is not unique to the victim mentality, it is definitely a key trait of this trap.

Naturally, this trait is easier to see in others than in ourselves. It is hard to actually witness ourselves going in circles. We just feel stuck. Nothing works and nothing helps.

Sometimes we say things like, "It hurts so much, I think I'm going to die!"

Are you really going to die?

We assure you that if you have not been physically harmed or diagnosed with a fatal ailment you can survive most if not all situations. You can sit with it, continue breathing and be gentle with yourself. What are you likely to be feeling while in a place of darkness?

Terror? Fear? Shame? Guilt?

These are emotions that can give any of us a feeling of being in a bottomless pit of emotional pain, feeling like death is upon us. We are not, however, dying when we have these feelings. We simply don't want to hear how to change our emotional state.

"It hurts so much. I think I'm going to die!"
Why do we say this?

We say this because if we did not have such a dramatic view, we would have to consider telling ourselves another story about what is really happening. Creating a new story would mean creating a better version of our life story, which may not fit into our current perspective.

Sometimes we say this:

"There is nothing that can be done; it's hopeless!"

But is that true?

In the movie, *La Vita è Bella (Life is Beautiful)*, Oscar award-winning actor Roberto Benigni portrays Guido Orefice, a Jewish father who, during World War II, is taken by the Nazis to a death camp along with his family. A disastrous situation. Men and women are separated. The father is housed with his young son. He uses his imagination to bring life and hope into what is one of the most hopeless situations of modern history. There is no guarantee of a positive outcome but it certainly shows us how to empower ourselves even in the most dire situations.

Every time we hear someone say to us,

"There is nothing that can be done; it's hopeless!"

We remember *La Vita è Bella*. We remember the beautiful concept of empowerment, using "choice" as our ticket out of total victimization.

You always have control over your thoughts. If nothing else, that's something you can work with to change your reality.

Needless to say, a person with victim consciousness would answer, *"Well, that's very nice, but that is just a movie."*

Or

"That's very nice, but I was not born with such strength. That is not something I can do. I'm not strong enough."

This way of thinking just lets one off the hook—but it also kills any chance of empowerment or possibilities. What do you choose to think: That there is no hope or that there are possibilities?

Victims feel a sense of lost worth.

Poor self-esteem is a definite trap and risk factor for the victim mentality.

We may believe we are defective. This belief can manifest itself after we have blamed everything around us and nothing regarding our situation has changed, thus we need to look elsewhere for blame. This belief is a distortion of reality. Being stuck, with a feeling of helplessness, does not mean that we are defective. It means that for now, we are feeling stuck or helpless. For now...

The Antidote

We can live for a few minutes or a few years in the victim mind-set but eventually we will grow weary of this landscape. Bit by bit, we can call ourselves back to our power and our true selves. The following strategies can be used as leverage against the victim mentality.

Be willing to let go of the idea that life must be a certain way.

We have all heard stories such as the Valentine's Day celebrations turning into nightmares because the twelve roses we received were the wrong color. Though it is more than OK to have preferences and boundaries, one still has to stay flexible enough to let life take its course.

Be willing to be flexible and be part of the flow of life.

Don't expect everything to be fair.

Just don't! Fairness is a cop-out. If you want give yourself five minutes (or five weeks) of whining about the unfairness of it all. We like to call this "the pity party." No problem—have a pity party—then pick yourself up and act on your best interests, leaving behind the *fairness* fairy tale.

Be willing to take responsibility for your own life and happiness.

Be your own hero! Take charge and take responsibility. You can only do what you can, but find out what that is, and do it!

Be honest about your feelings and take care of them.

Don't let negative feelings become your master. (According to *Star Wars*, that's exactly the moment you succumb to the dark side.)

You might be in the deepest emotional pain you've ever felt, a grief that paralyzes you… an anger that terrifies you… a shame that grips your heart and makes you feel sick inside…

Ask yourself what you will do about it.

Invite your nurturing side to come in and help with the emotion that is bringing you to your knees. If you cannot do it alone, seek outside counsel on what will help. In time, your feelings, hurts, and wounds will lessen and even heal if you are really there for yourself. If not, they will intensify.

Have some intellectual integrity.

Avoid negative inner or outer dialogue.

If you are neither in mortal danger nor diagnosed with a fatal illness, you are not dying. Even if you were in a life-threatening situation, it would be advisable to remain positive. Telling yourself and others your own story with added drama might feel like a release, but if you start to believe this version above all others you are creating a trap of powerlessness for yourself.

Cultivate gratitude and positive thinking.

When everything is gray that view can often be attributed to your outlook. Pick anything that is good and be sincere. It can be something very small, but feel your gratitude!

Gratitude has been shown in study after study to have an enormous impact on mood and to have the ability to immunize against depression and anxiety.

It does not matter what you are thankful for, be it hot water, a roof over your head, having enough to eat, or having a great love in your life. What matters is how deeply you feel this gratitude.

Foster resilience.

Resilience is a psychological concept. It is the ability to withstand difficult times. You can really fake this one until you integrate it. Can you survive storms? Might you try? Having resilience also requires letting go of control, trusting life and yourself to withstand challenges. The famous Serenity prayer says it best:

"God, grant me the serenity to accept the things I cannot change,

The courage to change the things I can,
And wisdom to know the difference." [4]

Exercise hope through what we know in Neuroscience.

We are only beginning to learn about our capacities. Neuroscience is offering us great hope for things that were considered impossible to do or to adjust not even a decade ago. The brain is capable of creating real change in your life with your ability to form new neuronal pathways through hopeful and positive thinking.

Accept help when it is genuinely offered to you.

Who says we are supposed to do everything alone?

We are social creatures. This is our strength. Let's be smart and accept help when it is genuinely offered from the heart. Women love to be superheroes and do it all themselves, while slowly falling apart. Our job is to take care of ourselves first so we can take care of the others we love. We cannot be there for others if we are not there for ourselves. Receiving help will allow us to stay more present for ourselves.

Live in the present moment.

When we worry about the future or obsess about the past we miss the chance to live our best lives. Such worry feeds victimization. Make the choice to live in the present. Living in the present doesn't mean you aren't looking after your future goals. It means being fully present in the moment, to be fully engaged in present conversations and activities.

The list of all the things you can do to ward off and heal victimization is long. Healing victimization is a way of living and so is the victim mind-set. You are in full control of what you chose to believe.

Believe in your worth.

Once you know your worth you cannot stay in the victim mind-set.

You were born worthy... You are always worthy

Martyr

Throughout history some of the world's most notable legitimate martyrs have been people like these:

Gandhi
Martin Luther King, Jr.
Mother Theresa

Those names show us that we are blessed to have been touched by the grace of these people as they changed the face of humanity.

To be as clear in one's beliefs as these people were, to be that strong in the face of adversity, holding one's position in order to carry the hopes of thousands or even millions is admirable beyond description.

When we see them in our mind's eyes, they are full of life, fiercely defending their beliefs and...*smiling!*

They all fit the Wikipedia definition of a martyr:

> "A **martyr** (Greek: μάρτυς, *mártys*, "witness"; stem μάρτυρ-, *mártyr-*) is somebody who suffers persecution and death for refusing to renounce, or accept, a belief or cause, usually religious."[5]

Being a martyr sounds like such a powerful thing to be, changing the world with one sacrifice after another. The world will change forever after your passage in history.

This mode of operation might work for a public figure when he or she is as strong as an oak, with a conviction that cannot be eroded by time, adversity, or critics—one who chooses the cause over his or her own comfort, welfare, and security and whose work touches a sea of people.

We may in our own way be saving world too by driving kids around, folding laundry, listening to a friend on the phone, forgiving someone for hurtful words, being supportive of our husbands, going to work and giving our best. These activities set the tone in our surroundings and affect the quality of life for people around us. If this is all done however, while we are feeling like we are "suffering persecution and death," then we have fallen into a dysfunctional version of martyrdom known as *the martyr complex*.

Why is it so easy to feel, from time to time (if not all the time for some of us), that we are stuck in to-do lists or to feel that there is not enough time on any given day to get everything done? Will our world crumble to the ground if we fail to build Rome in a day? We can most assuredly tell you it will not.

Why do we feel that we are indeed carrying the weight of the world on our shoulders?

We know we have been socialized that way—OK. But when does this socialization become a true martyr complex?

Martyr Complex

Wikipedia provides a clear description of the psychological trait known as the martyr complex:

> *In psychology, a person who has a* ***martyr complex****, sometimes associated with the term victim complex, desires the feeling of being a martyr for his/her own sake, seeking out suffering or persecution because it feeds a psychological need. In some cases, this results from the belief that the martyr has been singled out for persecution because of exceptional ability or integrity.* [6]

The martyr definitely has more power than the victim has. When we have the martyr complex, we accept a greater degree of responsibility and action than when we have the victim mind-set. Sometimes we will start by feeling victimized before moving to martyrdom. For some, that can be considered an "upgrade".

The martyr complex can be harvested from an overly strong sense of responsibility. The martyr is the ultimate "self-sacrificer." Self-sacrifice is expected of her and is sometimes even glorified. For the good of the family, for the good of the community, and in service to others, she is always present and always willing. That sounds good, doesn't it? We all would like to have a dutiful martyr on our side to support us.

Except when we do encounter our dutiful martyr, after a while (and it can take minutes or decades), the person starts to act a little differently.

Have you ever heard someone say this?

I cook for you! I suffer for you! What does it get me?
Do you know what I do for you?
Do you see what I do?
Everything is so difficult for me!

If so, you might have a martyr in front of you. Some of us might have to run to a mirror at this point. Yes, yes, let's not be shy; most of us have had, if not courted, the martyr complex at least from time to time.

Sense of Duty, Motherhood and Martyrdom

What is one of the most important roles a woman will play in her life? In all likelihood you answered mother?

You actually don't have to bear or raise children to admire and want to embody the mother archetype.

The nurturing, loving, and understanding nature that is a part of this universal feminine figure is very powerful. As a mother you have a unique role.

On so many levels, your presence is indispensable for the security and growth of your children. We know how much the nurturing touch is essential for complete brain and physical development. Research by Harry Frederic Harlow on rhesus monkeys is fascinating with respect to that topic. He demonstrated the importance of caregiving, touching, and companionship as keys to social and cognitive development. There is nothing like a mother's touch or the maternal instinct as a great defender and source of wisdom.

The Mother Archetype is often expected to be dutiful and without fault. Isn't that what we assumed of our own mothers in our formative years? We were entirely dependent on her for our wellness and survival. Quite often if she fails we will fail too.

This sense of duty can be tricky. The fragile nature of newborns demands a high level of commitment. The hours are long, with very little sleep to be had. The rest of the family still looks to moms for attention. Mothers who work outside the home feel a tremendous amount of pressure to become super employees or business owners refusing to let the added responsibilities from home affect their performance at work.

We forget that this picture is an archetype and not a real persona.

Nobody is only a mother. We are daughters, we are sisters, we are friends, we are girlfriends, we are wives, and most importantly we are women.

We are humans with needs!

If we construct our lives solely from a dutiful point of view, we will live flat, two-dimensional lives focused on completing tasks and gratifying the receivers of the tasks.

Dr. Jean Baker Miller, in her book, *Toward a New Psychology of Women*, stresses the particularly close relationship between women's upbringing and their sense of martyrdom:

> *"Women are taught that their main goal in life is to serve others—first men, and later, children. This prescription leads to enormous problems, for it is supposed to be carried out as if women did not have needs of their own, as if one could serve others without simultaneously attending to one's own interests and desires. Carried to its "perfection," it produces the martyr syndrome or the smothering wife and mother."*[7]

The duty of a mother is to care, nurture, and protect, but she has to be strong enough to do so. By consistently putting our own needs, wants and desires last, we inevitably fall into the martyr complex. Taken to its extreme form, a mother may eventually feel as if she has no needs of her own or what few needs she does have cannot be expressed.

We have travelled enough ground in our history as women to allow ourselves the right to look beyond the dutiful servant role given to us by society for over a millennia.

We often say to our clients, "Have you ever met a happy martyr?" We have not. So martyrdom is destined to lead to bitterness and frustration. Don't succumb to it!

The Inner Dialogue

Take a moment and think of the people whom you have seen embrace the role of martyr in their lives and think of the effect it had on them.

What we're talking about is self-sacrifice, which is often disguised as duty and commitment.

When we imagine a dutiful leader, we see her standing tall, with decisiveness in her eyes, her head held straight and strong.

When we see a *martyr-like* woman, however, she usually has rounded shoulders, a defeated expression with the clenched jaw of disappointment and a look of barely restrained anger in her eyes. Sometimes hardly breathing as she goes from task to task.

Indeed, sometimes we *feel* that we don't have a choice about certain chores that need to get done, but that's the key. It's a feeling, a learned emotion, and not a fact.

For example, it's ten o'clock at night and there is a pile of dirty dishes calling your name. You feel that those dishes have to be done.

But do you need to do them tonight or do them all by yourself?

What about doing the dishes tomorrow, asking your spouse or your older children for some help, or simply putting everything in the dishwasher (even those odd things that you have a rule about not putting in there) and turning it on? These are all choices you can make instead of engaging in the inner dialogue that compels you toward martyrdom.

Yes, yes, the answer is yes!
Those dishes have to be done now!
If I wait for tomorrow, I won't have time to do them!
I hate seeing dirty dishes in the morning!
My spouse never helps me with the dishes!
I would rather avoid his reaction, even if he does wash the dishes for me!
He won't even wash them properly anyway!
No, no! The pots never go in the dishwasher!

If you listen to this inner dialogue, what happens next? You go to your dishes with rounded shoulders, clenched jaw and a bitter taste about the task ahead of you, and all the chores of life in general. Maybe you're even harboring discontent about the people who dirtied the dishes…

All of these reactions occur because you habitually listen to the inner dialogue of martyrdom and you choose to respond accordingly. You just missed one key step.

You *chose* to have a clean kitchen now, even if you put it ahead of rest and sleep. *That's a choice! Your choice.*

Princesses of Inner Dialogue

One of the best examples of martyrdom in fairy tales is the story of "Beauty and the Beast."

Belle's self-sacrifice transforms the beast into a prince, so at least this fairy tale has the advantage of being a bit more complex than most—but more about that later.

Let's start with the prince, who is quite selfish. He is turned into a beast by a fairy, disguised as a woman in need of shelter and assistance. His face and body reflect the state of his heart: hard as stone and lacking empathy and regard for anyone else.

The prince seems to have the heart of a narcissist.

When the spell is cast upon him, he is told what the solution will be to remedy his affliction. Only by his finding true love, loving and being loved back despite his "*beasthood*" and ugliness, can the spell be broken, at which point he will regain his true form: his royal, princely "handsomeness."

Time passes by. A merchant comes to the castle in need of refuge. Upon his leaving he picks the most beautiful rose from the garden for his youngest daughter, Belle. (In the original version, Belle has two older sisters. They could be Cinderella's stepsisters, for all we know. They're petty, jealous, self- centered…oh, what the heck, why don't we bring them in on the stern lecture about women's solidarity that we gave the female characters in Cinderella's story?)

As he is leaving, the merchant comes face-to-face with the beast. The beast tells him that he must pay with his life for the transgression he committed by picking the rose in the garden, or he must send his beautiful daughter to pay his debt. Her life will be spared, but she will be held captive in the prince-beast's castle, and she must come willingly.

Of course our heroine is a perfectly dutiful daughter who sacrifices her freedom all because her father picked one rose to give to her.

Let's stress this again:

She sacrifices her freedom, all of her dreams and her future. She ***martyrs*** *herself to save another.*

She is patient. She loves. She understands. We believe that she has all the qualities of the mother archetype. It seems the prince needs to be re-parented in order to be saved, to be taught a good value system and to live accordingly. Belle does all of this selflessly. Of course it ends well. She has such a pure heart and is such a selfless being that her true love and purity touch the heart of the beast.

His royal "handsomeness" is restored, and forever-after happiness is secured.

The message sent to girls through this story is the essentially good and supportive nature of women has the power to turn the beast into a prince. (We feel a headache coming on at this point!)

Girls are also misled into believing that within feminine beauty and self-sacrifice lies the salvation of men. Men are enabled to change from beast to prince through no effort of their own. (Does this this mean if they don't change the fault is ours?)

To be clear, the message is that self-sacrifice brings healing to others, making you indispensable in their lives and bringing happiness for all. This is the hallmark of willful suffering in the name of duty.

What happens when this plan fails?
Is it the woman who should be blamed if the man remains a beast?
Was the woman not pretty enough?
Was she not understanding enough?
Not patient enough?
Was it that she just didn't comprehend what she was supposed to do to magically change this particular beast?
Did she not give enough of herself?
Did she not sacrifice enough of herself?
Was her love not pure enough to change the heart of the beast?

We must tell you quite frankly that the ending of this story is a lie. If a beastly man is getting all that he wants from a self-sacrificing woman, why would he change? A man will not be motivated to evolve as a person and treat you better when he is being spoilt by you. He will also not change when he has control over you. Why would he? This is true not only of men—this is human nature. So the question needs to be asked—why is it your job to fix him? Even though Belle suffered to save her father, why was it viewed as being her responsibility? Wasn't he in fact the one who had picked the rose when he was not supposed to? Is it a father's right to have his daughter pay for his errors? Is it a daughter's duty to carry the sins of her father? The subtexts are disturbing.

Another false message in this fairy tale is that Belle's self-sacrifice results in her happiness.

Really?

Have you ever met a happy martyr? Think of people you know who live their lives with a martyr mentality. Do they seem happy to you?

We have never met a happy martyr.

They only exist in fairy tales.

Stories don't tend to end well for the martyr. They're not supposed to.

Have you ever felt happy playing the martyr card? We certainly have not! It only starts the nagging internal voice about the sacrifices you've made, the injustice of it all, and how so many people are insensitive and don't even notice or care. When the whole world starts to *be wrong* and just simply seems to be off somehow, you should look inward. You might even want to look at your face in the mirror when you have played the martyrdom card for a while; you'll notice that you look worried, defeated, and quite annoyed, if not overtly aggressive.

If you choose to live the martyr fairy tale in real life then you should do so in full awareness of the consequences. *Martyrdom is a self-fulfilling prophecy of sacrifice.* If you use this tool in the hope of being glorified, loved, and appreciated, the chances are that this will not happen. More likely you will lose the twinkle in your eyes, the smile on your face and your self-esteem.

The Deeper River

The self-sacrificing woman is unhappy and relinquishes responsibility for her *own* well-being. The martyr continuously sacrifices herself for a cause.

Ironically, when the martyr feels responsible for everything and everyone around her, she fails to be responsible for herself. Despite all her hard work she remains unhappy and unfulfilled.

She fuels a latent and ever-increasing source of anger and frustration inside, which can lead to feelings of helplessness and despair.

In a pattern similar to that of the victim, she feels she is not responsible for the pain she struggles to keep at bay.

She blames other things, whether they are circumstances or people, as being responsible for her misery. The reality is that she has allowed them to have the ability to affect her.

The dance of blame and guilt is fierce in the martyr's heart. Effort and painful sacrifices should change the face of the earth! (Right? Wrong.)

She is stuck.

She is quite unhappy. She works so very hard!

She perceives herself as being surrounded by selfish people who don't sacrifice as much as she does, and they seem unable to recognize the value of her work and her sacrifices. She is hoping to appear as someone who needs to be rescued from her situation, and for a time, she might be. But the cycle of self-sacrifice will not end that way. Like a shadow lurking and waiting, it can rest for a time, waiting for another crisis to appear. When hardship knocks on the door, the martyr answers in anticipation, eager to show her capabilities again.

External approval is such a powerful reinforcer.

Sometimes we are indeed searching for this approval more than for love or happiness. We'll give up anything for that approval. When this happens, we have stepped into the realm of martyrdom, and because we have not taken care of ourselves, we are depleted.

That is still not the end of it. What and who completes a martyr's self-fulfilling mind-set? Who benefits from you putting yourself last?

Since you do and give so-o-o-o much, you will inevitably seek relationships with people who gladly take so-o-o-o much from you. Especially if you are handing it to them with no questions asked.

The worst part is that for the deal to be completely sealed the taker will believe he (or she) deserves so-o- o-o much that he will actually demand what you are have been giving so freely.

In our concepts of grandeur, our egos kick in and we convince ourselves we are the ones who can give the most (we might even be the only ones who can give what we are giving) and we will prove it. We will therefore unknowingly attract someone who also has grand ideas about himself, but for this person, it is more about what he deserves from the world and from you.

Have you guessed who the martyr dances with? Here is a hint. Who was the beast in "Beauty and the Beast," before he was changed into beastly form?

He was a narcissistic prince!

Egoism, selfishness, self-absorption—does this describe anybody in your life? Do you end up running around doing his or her bidding instead of living your own life? If yes, then you are indeed dancing this special dance of the martyr with the narcissist.

The hardest part of accepting this is realizing that your willingness to do too much is part of the problem. It's an airtight system. The martyr *overfunctions* and the narcissist *underfunctions*. Since it takes two to tango, you are both part of the problem. The good news is you are also both part of the solution.

It is important to understand this, because the people you will dance with in martyrdom will, most of the time, be close to you. The person(s) can be your spouse, your kids, your parents, your friends, your coworkers, your boss…

This is especially significant to consider if you are a parent. You do not want to initiate and cultivate a martyr/narcissist dance with your kids. This one is a very easy slippery slope for most women to fall into. If it seems as though you are raising self-absorbed little people, it is more than time to look at what you overdo for them and what drives you to do so.

It will be impossible for your kids not to do the martyr/narcissist dance with you if you are interacting with them as a martyr!

The good news is this dance can be changed. Just as one adopts the martyr complex as a way of living, it is not one's definite, unchangeable personality trait. Generally, the other person's narcissistic behavior can be changed as well. This is important to know. But let's be clear: the narcissist is getting so much out of this deal; don't expect him or her to be the first to change the music. Why would they? Change the dance yourself.

When one travels the road of martyrdom, the sense of self and empowerment is lacking, and thus, one's vitality is diminished. Resentment, blame and guilt run deep. In the end we are responsible and sometimes too responsible, because we are too involved when we need not be. We end up attracting the wrong people or the wrong behavior in people.

At the core of every martyr's mentality one thing is missing: the knowledge that each of us is individually responsible for his or her own well-being, growth and happiness.

Be responsible for your own self! When you avoid this responsibility—that is when you slip into the trap of martyrdom.

Payoffs

What is truly going on within the mind of the martyr? What is beneath the surface? Since we now know this strategy ends up in misery, why is it so prevalent? Although not obvious, it is quite likely because there are many payoffs!

Being the One:

Martyrdom gives a person the elated feeling of being "the one."

The act of self-sacrifice can give us a sense of "exceptional ability or integrity." When we entertain the belief *that only we can do something because no one else will*, we perceive ourselves as being special.

If we work this hard at being special we probably feel at a subconscious level that we are not. Why else would we need our specialness to be proclaimed?

If we knew how special and unique we are, if we knew with absolutely certainty that no one else in the world is like us and never will be, if we had true self-esteem and confidcncc, believing in ourselves with any degree of assuredness, we wouldn't have to work so hard to prove it to others.

From the martyr's perspective, self-sacrifice is the best way to is to achieve a sense of being "*the special one.*"

Extraordinary gestures.
A mountain of effort.
A selfless cause.
Surely you will be proclaimed!

If that doesn't work, martyrs can always fall back on self-proclaiming:

"Look at all the effort I give!"

A third alternative is to accuse someone else of being less than… (less than you, of course).

"Look at how lazy he is!"

Getting Sympathy

If martyrdom doesn't give you the recognition of being seen as "the special one" or "the big hero", then surely the amount of effort you exhibit will attract you masses of sympathy. This is a very seductive side of the martyr role.

When you provide significant effort, even when it has been proven again and again that the effort does not yield the results you expected, ask yourself, "*what my payoff?*" Are you looking to resolve "the problem" or are you looking for "sympathy". Which of these two will bring you the validation you require.

Playing the Blame Game

The martyr typically blames others for their own lack of happiness. Just like the victim, the martyr avoids responsibility for him/herself. Martyrdom creates a very complex set of circumstances where the person will feel overly responsible, but for the wrong things and people.

Since the martyr puts so much effort into what she does, taking care of countless things and people, no matter how things are unfolding, she cannot and will not take responsibility for any of it. After all, she has given *all* that she has.

Since the martyr sees herself as such a heroic and selfless figure, she will often put a vast amount of effort in the wrong place in order to avoid responsibility. Often blaming others for situations that seem to be getting out hand.

*"Let the responsibility fall on someone else's shoulders;
I have enough on my own!"*

*"If only my luck would change, with all the effort I put forth,
I would be on top for sure!"*

Playing Smother me; Smother Me Not

Another perverse side of this glorified form of self-sacrifice is created with the expectation that in return for the sacrifice the martyr expects the same level of sacrifice as an acceptable and desirable behavior.

Happiness is not part of the equation. This is not a win-win situation, but rather a *lose-lose* deal.

This is closer to hatred than love. "I've sacrificed my happiness, my well-being and my growth. I expect you to do the same."

Within the martyrdom mind-set, you as the martyr have bled yourself so much that you believe you own the right to demand the sacrifices and the effort of others.

Again, reciprocity is essential in relationships, but so are boundaries and sometimes enough is enough.

If you live with the mind-set that you are not responsible for yourself and are willing to bleed and sacrifice yourself for others, and as a result are not willing to take care of yourself, then you are not in reciprocity land, but in martyrdom kingdom!

The Antidote

This section is for those of you who have identified yourselves as martyrs. What can you do to get yourself out of the martyr mindset? Is change possible? We urge you to try and keep an open mind. Change is entirely possible with some will-power and daily effort. We hope you will try some or all of the steps below to move along the process:

Ask yourself, "Am I over the top?"

Are you overdoing it? Can you identify areas in your life where you are over-functioning, taking on too much responsibility or assuming too much control? Take a moment to think about this and then write them down.

Remember, over-functioning invites people with narcissistic personalities to you. You are offering to take on responsibility- they are looking to get rid of responsibility. The dance begins...

Over-functioners attract under-functioners. You will probably see them as selfish and you might very well be right. If you are not willing to let go of your over-functioning part, it is very unlikely they will let go of their part of the dance. Once you've decided to stop over functioning be prepared for some resistance. If you have given your loved ones a sweet deal for any amount of time it's quite normal for them to struggle with any changes in behavior or routine. Do not despair, this is normal. Keep your resolution!

Speak the truth to yourself.

Be willing to ask yourself tough questions about what is motivating your behavior.

Ask yourself, "Am I putting on my 'suffering hat' because I want them to feel badly for me right now so that I can get my way with something?" Quite often there is more at play when we consciously or unconsciously put on our suffering hats. Have you ever asked yourself why you are angry or frustrated with someone? Are you really frustrated with them or are you frustrated with what their behavior reminds you of? Is it time to address the situation head on with the person involved or is it time to accept that you should simply "let go".

Become aware of why you do what you do. Write down some typical scenarios in your life and face them honestly. Vow to make different choices beginning today.

Choice!

You will find true empowerment and release from the bonds of martyrdom by taking responsibility for yourself and by acknowledging that you must own your choices. Don't wait for perfection, don't wait to be completely certain and don't wait to feel it's easy enough. Choose today! Especially if that means choosing the lesser of two evils—choose! Once you have made your choice, walk yourself mentally through your process

"I really don't feel like going to my in laws-this weekend, but its little Abby's birthday. I feel I have to go."

HALT!
You could in fact not go.

"Yes, but that choice would make me feel bad and cheap!"
"Yes, but I would rather avoid those feelings and also not disappoint Abby..."

So your choices are:
Not going, even if it means you will feel bad and Abby might be disappointed.

- Or -

Going to the party even if you don't feel like it.

Just because you don't like any of the choices in front of you, doesn't mean they are not indeed choices, because they are.

Exercise your power of choice and take a minute to notice this is indeed a choice. Furthermore, it is *your choice.*

Count your blessings and reciprocities.

If you are in a relationship where mutual reciprocity is out of balance, then you are on a slippery slope toward martyrdom or victimization. Check the reciprocity in your relationship. There must be reciprocity for relationships to work. Know when you are in dangerous territory.

Recognize yourself, your talents and your effort.

If your Achilles' heel is external approval, look inward for self-motivation and inspiration. Start having a dialogue with *yourself.* Take the time to notice yourself, including your efforts, your talents and your worth.

Accept your limits.

If you are asking too much of yourself, you are your own worst enemy.

I'm human, you're human. And we all have limits. Know them and respect them.

Remember: Happiness is not part of the equation.

If martyrdom grips you, and you are going in circles in your mind, remember this:

There are no happy martyrs.

With time, this little truth will make its way into your very being. You will be drawn less and less toward choosing the martyrdom way. Even if you need to make tough choices you will know that you have a better chance of succeeding and increasing your happiness quota if you choose another road other than the path of martyrdom and victimhood.

Take responsibility for yourself, for your happiness and for your well-being!

Caretaker

The disease of caretaking is one we became fascinated with many years ago. We have alluded to it throughout this book as it leaks into both victimization and martyrdom complex.

We both grew up thinking that caretaking meant being kind, and being kind was strongly reinforced in our families. We suspect that it was in yours too. Why do we say this? Well, because caretaking is considered a highly valued female quality. We are, after all, the mothers of our societies, the ones who make sure our families run smoothly and the ones who tend to look after our mates. As women and mothers our role has always been to care for those in our immediate surroundings and in large part, the community. **So what is the problem?**

There are big problems with caretaking.

Caretaking literally means assuming the mental and physical well-being of another. There are professional caretakers—therapists, nurses, and doctors, for instance but it is important to note that professional caretakers are paid for their services, making their relationships with their patients reciprocally beneficial. Without this reciprocity, these relationships would quickly slip into dysfunction. This is the same problem we saw with martyrs.

Healthy Adult relationships are based on reciprocity.

Caretaking another without this healthy balance is often referred to as *Codependency*. It is not healthy to keep giving to another with the hope of change (caretakers always are caretaking to (unconsciously perhaps) elicit some sort of change or control the outcome of a situation).

As Marlene M. Maheu puts it, "Codependency is a type of relationship where an individual gives of themselves, even when they do not want to, or shouldn't for their own welfare." [8]

So why do people caretake when they are not paid professionals?

Control:

The sad fact is that while there are payoffs to being a caretaker, these payoffs are ultimately very dysfunctional. One of the key payoffs is control. The theory goes like this: If I take care of another person, I gain the illusion of control. I am going to get that person to do what I want him or her to do. Although this situation rarely maintains itself, at first it seems that the caretaking is gaining you exactly what you want. Then suddenly, one day, you realize that the person/thing/situation you thought you were controlling is controlling you.[9] You find yourself obsessing and strategizing to make sure the "other" does what you think would be best while they are "chilling out"... From their perspective why stress? They have you there to stress for them. What has gone wrong here? Who is controlling who?

Temporary high:

Another significant payoff for caretakers is it temporarily inflates one's self-esteem. The reasoning is that I must be very important if I am showing someone else the right way to do things and thus showing the person the errors of his or her ways. Sadly, this kind of "drug hit" is short-lived and is not a real source of self-esteem.

Caretaking that involves one-sided giving and receiving nothing in return is almost a type of addictive behavior that is bound to cause problems.

It is in essence, taking on an "I know better" position disguised as kindness or helpfulness. Even a professional caretaker such as a therapist must be paid for his or her services. Why? If the help given by the caretaker is not reciprocated (in this case) in the form of payment, then it becomes one sided and thus dysfunctional. This goes for all adult relationships- one sided giving does not ultimately work. Why is this?

When one person is giving and the other only receiving, what happens eventually to each one of them? The *giver* eventually becomes very resentful and quite depleted. The *receiver* becomes.... overfed, *spoilt* and over-entitled. This is neither a good dance nor a healthy one in any kind of relationship.

If you are dancing this dance- it is time to change the dance.

Many of you might be questioning what is wrong with just being kind to another? Being kind to another is perfectly healthy and even to be encouraged. But kindness is NOT caretaking.

Caretaking vs Kindness

Let's first distinguish between caretaking and acts of kindness toward people you love. Caretakers tend to think they know what is best for others and that is part of what motivates them to "help." This is the beginning of a slippery slope, as healthy relationships are based on knowing that that you only know what is best for yourself. When you rob someone of going on their own journey, bumps and all- you are not in kindness, you are in caretaking.

A big clue that you have fallen into caretaking is that caretaking is exhausting and tends to deplete you, whereas kindness actually feels energizing.

One of the safest ways of knowing whether you have slipped into caretaking is to check whether your cup is full, so to speak. Have you attended to your own needs and desires before "helping" someone else? If you have, you will feel great. If you have not attended to your basic needs but instead are helping someone else, you will undoubtedly display symptoms of exhaustion, anxiety, or depression, or even symptoms of physical ailments. *Does this speak to you?*

A true caretaker will think taking care of her needs first as being selfish. The truth, however, is that taking care of your own needs allows you to be of greater service to the world and to the people around you.

The famous "oxygen mask" on an airplane comes to mind: You must put the oxygen mask on yourself first before you can be of help to anyone else (even your own child). In day to day operations once you take care of yourself, you are happy and healthy because your needs are being met, and thus you can really be of help to others, not only in direct ways but also by role modeling what happy and healthy looks like.

Caretaking and relationships:

Interestingly, true caretaking women tend to attract needy personality types; they are a natural draw. You lovingly rescue the needy, wounded person, and initially, your self-esteem gets a boost. Sadly, this boost is similar to a drug hit, and as with all addictions, such behavior is not healthy, and you will need more and more hits (more rescues) as you go along.

At the beginning of the relationship the needy, wounded person will demonstrate tremendous gratitude to you for revealing the error of his or her ways. As the relationship begins to mature the person in the role of the "cared for" will slowly but surely become furious with you for meddling in his or her business. When that day comes, you will be deeply hurt because of all you have done for that person. You will realize that your relationship with that person was created out of the subtle yet toxic nature of caretaking and not necessarily out of love.

Caretaking is often referred to in Psychological literature as Co-dependency.

A big clue to determining whether you tend towards codependency/caretaking is to see whether you jump to fix other people's problems and unconsciously foster dependence. Healthy, non-caretaking responses to a problem will just simply involve empathizing with the problem and allowing the other person to solve it in whatever manner they deem fit (even if you think you know better). **It is their journey** to figure out what works and what does not. Ironically, the true caretaker unconsciously likes the dependence created, as it gives the illusion that she/he will not be abandoned by the other person, and yet the emptiness that this kind of relationship creates is far worse than the original fear. Further, if all your relationship choices are based on avoiding abandonment- what happens to you in that equation? *You have already been abandoned*... **by yourself.**

You don't have to abandon yourself to be kind to others. As a matter of fact you are engaging in true kindness you feel good. When you are caretaking, you walk away rolling your eyes, sighing and usually grumbling about not being appreciated.

To thine own self be true...

Secret Wish of Caretaking

Have you ever wondered what caretakers secretly long for? Have you ever wondered about the motivation of a caretaker? Let's begin with the premise that humans are not selfless. We may do acts of selflessness but we are not selfless in that we do good things to feel good (which still gives us something in return for our act of kindness). So if we are not inherently selfless, and yet we are involved in continual caretaking, what do we want in return?

The secret wish of caretakers is...*to be taken care of.* It makes sense—as humans we often give what we would like to receive. The sad reality is that caretaking does not invite being taken care of. It actually invites exploitation. This may be surprising to learn. If this is something you've struggled with, maybe you are disappointed in yourself more than surprised.

Be encouraged, the cycle can be broken today!

The Antidote

So what actually happens when you fall into the trap of dysfunctional caretaking (and we do not mean being kind—we mean caretaking)? To put it simply, the other person gets his/her cup filled, but what happens to your cup? If your cup is full to begin with, you are not caretaking, you are engaging in kindness and generosity, and it will make you feel happy and invigorated rather than depleted. Sadly, most caretakers have very empty pockets. Many are exhausted, bitter, and often showing symptoms of anxiety, depression, or physical illness. Remarkably, the people they are obsessively taking care of, albeit troubled, thrive under the attention they are receiving.

The entire dynamic of a caretaking relationship revolves around an over-functioning partner (often the woman, though not always) with an under-functioning mate or counterpart (the under-functioner can be your growing child). The most frustrating part is that the caretaker, through the illusion of control, believes that the under-functioner will step up to the plate sooner or later. The problem is that as long as the under-functioning person in the relationship is being fed so much attention, why on earth would that person change his or her ways?

So it is time to fill up your pockets. How do you replenish? What do you do to show your own importance to yourself? Make yourself your own project and the dynamics of your relationship will naturally change. You are important. Put that oxygen mask on yourself first!

Balance: Where Do You Give Your Attention?

A question you might want to ask yourself to determine whether or not you are slipping out of balance is: Am I giving as much to myself as I am giving to any particular relationship? How is the reciprocity factor going in my relationships? If it seems out of balance, you know you need to come back to self-care. Also consider what this imbalance is creating in your relationship:

In the field of psychology, reinforcement is considered a key factor as to why people do the things they do. One of the biggest reinforcements of all is *attention*, negative or positive. When the act of caretaking is done with the hope that a change in behavior will occur in the one being cared for, the result is often disastrous. The change will probably never happen. As a caretaker you are simply encouraging the victim mindset. The person being cared for is being reinforced in his or her helpless or even hopeless ways. For many the state of being cared for is far too enjoyable to deny. Why would the person want to change that?

Where do you put your attention? What we give attention to grows, even bad behaviors, will be reinforced.

True caretakers have personality types that naturally and quite easily neglect the self. The question is why? They are too busy caretaking and controlling their environment. Ironically, the person being taken care of does not grow or heal his or her issues. This is because caretaking keeps the receiver of the care in a position of continual dependence and growth can only be achieved through one's own belief in one's own ability to handle life's trials and tribulations.

When a caterpillar is in its cocoon, it needs to struggle to get out and become a butterfly. If you help the caterpillar out of the cocoon, it usually will die. If you let it struggle, it will come out when the time is right and grow into a beautiful butterfly.

Let go…

Humans are the same. When we take the struggle out of someone's hands, we enable the person to stay stuck in the cocoon. They start to feel they will "die" without us which might appeal to our ego but is hardly healthy. We are interfering with the person's process. When we allow the person the opportunity to sort out his or her issues and break out of the cocoon, they have the opportunity to become a butterfly. If he or she does not, it's doubtful you could have saved them. In some ways we are on a lonely journey. We cannot save others. As experienced practitioners we can assure you people save themselves… let them.

So what is the cure for caretaking? Are we meant to become selfish narcissists? Throughout our years of practice many of our clients have been very concerned about this.

Good News/Bad News

Caretakers are the nicest people you will ever meet. The guru on caretaking codependent behaviors, Melodie Beattie, highlights this concept in her life-changing book, *Codependent No More*, a must read for anyone struggling with this issue. The good news regarding these personality types is that they really cannot become selfish narcissists, but that is also part of the bad news. Caretaking is a tendency that at best gets managed not cured.

Other women, mothers, wives, daughters and society in general will attempt to put us back into the role of caretaker time and again *if we let them.*

Furthermore, we might be shamed or made to feel guilty if we do not accept this role. But it is not an all-or-nothing concept. You can be nice, and you can stay loving and considerate. To change the dysfunctional pattern of excessive caretaking you have to ask yourself some serious questions and be ready to reframe your state of mind.

Whatever you are giving out to others, are you giving to yourself?

Be honest now. Remember the concept of attention. Do you give yourself the same amount of attention that you afford the person you are trying to help or control? If the answer is no, you are in a dysfunctional relationship that can only become dangerous. A good way of tracking this is to think about this in terms of an "empty pocket" theory. Can you give a dollar to someone when your pockets are empty? No. Giving your love, attention, and care to another person when you have not given to yourself is like giving a dollar from an empty pocket. *You are giving what you do not have.*

Not only is that completely depleting to you but how can it possibly be considered taking good, proper care of another? It actually sends a mixed message. You yourself are not walking the walk and yet you are asking someone else to do just that.

*Walk the walk...**your own walk.***

Do you think you know best?

If you are operating from a position of knowing what is best for others, you are veering off in the direction of dysfunctional caretaking, right into full-fledged codependency, and you are definitely not acting in kindness. We only know what is best for ourselves. Only trained professionals can give unbiased advice on what might be best for someone else, and even then, only when the advice is solicited by that person.

It is not our job to teach others the errors of their ways…

One of the most empowering things you can do for others is to trust their ability to solve their own problems. Take a moment to examine yourself. Do you believe the person in question can deal with his or her own life, or have you fallen into the "savior complex," where you believe that only you can save the person? We assure you, even as trained professionals who have worked with and been credited with helping hundreds of people, we know a secret: We did not save them; **they ultimately saved themselves.** While trained professionals can guide and coach, the actual change comes from the person themselves. Furthermore even trained therapists cannot "therapize" anyone who is not a "formal" client or they are flirting with codependency too.

Let people sort out their own journeys.

Ultimately, people save themselves… or not.

Questions to Ask Yourself to Immunize Against Caretaking Fallout

Have you been feeling symptoms of anxiety or depression lately?

Feeling anxious or depressed might be a symptom alerting you that you might have fallen into caretaking. Giving with empty pockets and with an exaggerated sense of responsibility lends itself to anxiety and/or depression symptoms.

Do you have a preponderance of "needy" people around you?

Caretaking attracts people with problems, so if you find yourself wondering why everyone comes to you with his or her problems, you have probably fallen into the trap of caretaking. Caretakers attract needy people who have fallen into victimhood as both parties feed off of each other (dysfunctionally). Proceed with caution.

"If anyone tries to complicate your life, turn and walk away from them." Caroline Myss[10]

Do you clearly know the difference between empathizing with someone and fixing someone?

Fixing someone is getting into a dance with him or her, and it is definitely caretaking/codependent. Empathizing with someone's problems is healthy, not an energy zapper and it allows the person to find his or her own solutions.

The expression, "Love thy neighbor as you would yourself," implies that you will love yourself first. Hear it again: "*Love your neighbor as you would yourself.*" How is your love affair going with yourself?[11] If you find yourself feeling a bit uneasy at this question, then the chances are there is not exactly a love affair going on with yourself. Many of our clients find the concept of having love relationships with themselves a bit boring. Having said that, they often complain and are upset about why their lives are lacking in external love.

Many years ago, Sandra coined an equation that is now known as the "Reich" equation:

The love outside of yourself is directly proportionate to the love you give yourself.

Let's take that in for a few moments longer.

The love outside of yourself is directly proportionate to the love you give yourself.

How much love are you giving yourself?

If not much, then how much love can come to you?

Caretakers are busy caretaking others and not loving themselves, and yet caretakers, like all people, crave to be loved and dedicate a lot of effort to getting love.

This formula will only lead to self-defeat.

Self- love combined with self-care is **the** pathway to feeling the secure peaceful feelings that caretakers and actually all humans crave.

You might need to practice it to master it.

Homework

Make a list of loving behaviors you will do for yourself on a weekly basis, and if possible, on a daily basis: Write down what makes you feel loved.

These behaviors could involve taking, journaling, affirmations or any other idea you are drawn to that represents of self-care. For some people enhancing the practice might include some type of spiritual work, meditating, exercising, or expressing yourself, creatively through art, music, or crafts. Make a list of ways you can build these self-affirming, caring activities into your daily life. **You are important.**

You are important; your life and your behaviors must reflect that in order for you or anyone else to believe that.

We assure you that if you really live true to the concept of loving yourself fully, with the same reverence you give to caretaking another, you'll feel outstanding. You will also draw into your life the same level of love and appreciation from others that you are finally giving to yourself. Furthermore, when you come across people who are struggling and whom you naturally want to help, you will remember that you have given them the greatest gift of all: **a role model.**

You must be the change you wish to see in the world.
Mahatma Gandhi

Concluding Thoughts

The road to empowerment is very special. It is filled with potholes, with crevices full of challenges, and yet it is also filled with healing.

We know relationships are designed to heal you. We don't like pain, no one does however it is through pain that we usually find healing.

We need to reflect again on the caterpillar's journey toward becoming a butterfly. When the caterpillar completes its struggle, it becomes a beautiful, unique butterfly. Without the struggle, the caterpillar dies, never having fulfilling its destiny.

Women's unseen radiance is much like this. We have struggled, and we continue to struggle, but our radiance grows each time we come out of our cocoons. Our butterflies are stronger and more radiant with each generation and particularly as we understand more about ourselves.

There is much to learn and much to say. *Once Upon a Time: How Cinderella Grew Up and Became an Empowered Woman* is only part one of a series that will include much more about empowering women, enhancing relationships and reaching for the stars.

The book has been a labor…of love. We will continue to write, teach, and empower women as each and every one of you continues to inspire us. You are all our sisters in the journey—not always an easy journey—and we are honored to work with you. We love the stories you share at our workshops. We are deeply touched by the raw honesty and courage we see time and time again in our fellow women on those special days and weekends. Thank you for encouraging us to start writing our insights down and thank you for joining us on the ride.

Welcome to Empowerment and Empowered Women Workshops. Come and see us at one of our workshops or retreats (www.empoweredwomenworkshops.com), or drop us a line at empoweredwomenmtl@hotmail.com and tell us about your journey. We would love to hear from you or, better yet, to meet you.

Sandra and Maïté

And You Lived, You Truly Lived!

From the core of your being and from the depths of who you truly are, you can live! You can fully live!
Through ups and downs, but such a rich life, you can live, always diving into your deeper, truer selves.
It is indeed a wonderful, full, ecstatic and humbling, real and loving, ever growing and expanding journey.
What say you?
You decided to experience and taste life! This is just the beginning.

What you can choose is to live life fully, to be present with all of what makes you who you are, knowing this is truly what makes a difference!
Be fully aware that you didn't need to have a perfect story, because you feel the flow of life going through you. You can let it dance with your true self, and that is enough to make your heart sing…

Your happily ever after is and has always been available to you. From within, from the core of your true self.

In loving yourself, you can find the authenticity of being and the excitement of discovering life!
The journey continues: keep your eyes on the stars!

Maïté and Sandra

Empowered Women Workshops
www.empoweredwomenworkshops.com

Notes

1. Marianne Williamson, *A Return to Love: Reflections on the Principles of A Course in Miracles* (Harper Collins, 1992), 190–191.
2. Steve Harvey, *Act Like a Lady Think Like a Man* (New York: HarperCollins, 2009), 150–152.
3. *Wiktionary, s.v.* "Victim", last modified on 10 February 2014, http://en.wiktionary.org/wiki/victim
4. *Wikipedia*, s.v. "Serenity Prayer," last modified May 3, 2013, http://en.wikipedia.org/wiki/Serenity_Prayer.
5. *Wikipedia*, s.v., "Martyr," last modified May 27, 2013, http://en.wikipedia.org/wiki/Martyr.
6. *Wikipedia*, s.v. "Martyr Complex," last modified May 14, 2013, http://en.wikipedia.org/wiki/Martyr_complex.

7. Jean Baker Miller, *Toward a New Psychology of Women* (Boston: Beacon Press, 1976), 62.
8. Marlene M. Maheu, selfhelpmagazine.com, Co-Dependency or Kindness? Originally published 5/29/98 Revised 04/27/2009 by Marlene M. Maheu, Ph.D.
9. Melody Beattie, *Codependent No More* (Minnesota: Hazeldon Foundation, 1987) 75-78.
10. "Carolyne Myss," date posted February 2nd 2010, retrieved from http://forums.myss.com/ubbthreads.php?ubb=showflat&Number=137666
11. Melody Beattie, *Codependent No More* (Minnesota: Hazeldon Foundation, 1987) 119-122.

Bibliography

Beattie, Melody, *Codependent No More: How to Stop Controlling Others and Start Caring for Yourself,* Hazelden Foundation, Minnesota, 1987.

Beck, Martha, *the Joy Diet 10 Daily Practices for a Happier Life,* Crown Publishers, New York, 2003.

Bolte Taylor Ph.D., Jill, *My Stroke of Insight, A Brain Scientist's Personal Journey,* Penguin Group, New York, 2006.

Borysenko Ph.D., Joan, *A Woman's Book of Life, the Biology, psychology, and Spirituality of the Feminine Life Cycle,* Berkley Publishing Group, New York, 1996.

Bradshaw, John, *Home Coming Reclaiming and Championing Your Inner Child,* Bantam, USA, 1992.

Burns, M.D., David, *The Feeling Good Handbook,* Penguin Books, New York, 1999.

Chopra, Deepak, *The Path to Love: Spiritual Strategies for Healing*, Three Rivers Press, New York, 1997.

Chopra, Deepak, *The Seven Spiritual Laws of Success*, Co-published by Amber-Allen Publishing and New World Library, San Rafael, 1994.

Choquette, Sonia, *Traveling at the Speed of Love*, Hay House, USA, 2010.

Dyer, Wayne W., *Excuses Be Gone!: How to Change Lifelong, Self-Defeating Thinking Habits,* Hay House Inc., Printed in the United State of America, 2009.

Dyer, Wayne W., *The Power of Intention: Learning to Co-create Your World Your Way*, Way Hay House Inc., Printed in the United State of America, 2009.

Gottman, Ph.D., John M. and Joan DeClaire, *The Relationship Cure, A 5 Step Guide to Strengthening Your Marriage, Family, and Friendships*, Three Rivers Press, New York, 2001.

Hanson, Ph.D. Rick, and Menius MD., Richard, *the practical neuroscience of Buddha's Brain, happiness, love & wisdom,* New Harbinger Publication, Oakland, 2009.

Harvey, Steve, *Act Like a Lady Think Like a Man,* HarperCollins Publisher, New York, 2009

Hay, Louise L., *Heal Your Body*, Hay House, Carlsbad, 1982.

Hendrix Ph.D., Harville, *Getting the Love You Want, A guide For Couples,* Holt Paperbacks, New York, 1988.

Hicks, Esther and Jerry, *Ask and It Is Given, Learning to Manifest Your Desires,* Hay House, Carlsbad, 2004.

Johanson, Greg and Kurtz, Ron, *Grace Unfolding Psychotherapy in the Spirit of the Toa-te ching*, Harmony Books New York, 1991.

Katie, Byron, *I Need Your Love—Is That True?*, Random House, News York, 2005.

Lesser, Elisabeth, *Broken Open, How Difficult Times Can Help Us Grow,* Villard Books, New York, 2004.

Myss Ph. D., Caroline, *Anatomy of the Spirit: the Seven Stages of Power and Healing,* Three River Press, New York, 1996.

Paul, Margaret, *Inner Bonding: Becoming a Loving Adult to Your Inner Child*, HarperCollins Publisher, New York, 1990.

Robins, Anthony, *Awaken The Giant Within, How to take immediate control of your mental, emotional, physical & financial destiny!*, Free Press, New York, 2003.

Ruiz, Don Miguel, *The Four Agreements, A Practical Guide to Personal Freedom*, Amber-Allen Publishing Inc., San Rafael, 1997

Vanzan, Iyanla, *Peace from Broken Pieces, How to get Through What You're Going Through,* SmileyBooks, New York, 2010.

Williamson, Marianne, *A Return to Love: Reflections on the Principles of A Course in Miracles*, HarperCollins Publisher, New York, 1992.

Winfrey, Oprah, *The Oprah Show*, ABC, Chicago, from 1986 to 2011.

60174844R00075

Made in the USA
Charleston, SC
26 August 2016